W9-AUZ-613

Pasta

Pasta

SIMPLE, PERFECT RECIPES FOR MOUTHWATERING PASTA DISHES

Love Food™ is an imprint of Parragon Books Ltd

Parragon Publishing
Queen Street House
4 Queen Street
Bath BA1 1HE, UK

Copyright © Parragon Books Ltd 2008

Love Food™ and the accompanying heart device is a trademark of Parragon Books Ltd

All rights reserved. No part of this publication may be reproduced, stored in a retrieval
system, or transmitted, in any form or by any means, electronic, mechanical, photocopying,
recording, or otherwise, without the prior permission of the copyright holder.

ISBN: 978-1-4075-3297-4

Printed in China

Cover design by Andrew Easton at Ummagumma

Notes for the Reader
This book uses imperial, metric, or US cup measurements. Follow the same units of
measurement throughout; do not mix imperial and metric. All spoon measurements are
level: teaspoons are assumed to be 5 ml, and tablespoons are assumed to be 15 ml.
Unless otherwise stated, milk is assumed to be whole, eggs and individual vegetables
such as potatoes are medium, and pepper is freshly ground black pepper. Recipes using
raw or very lightly cooked eggs should be avoided by infants, the elderly, pregnant women,
convalescents, and anyone suffering from an illness.

There is surely no other food that could be simpler. Pasta, the national dish of Italy is now eaten all over the world. It is made from durum wheat flour and water, and sometimes enriched with egg or oil. Although it may be one of the simplest of foods, it is probably the most varied. It comes in over 650 different shapes and sizes, and can be flavored by herbs, spinach, or tomato. Pasta can be prepared by hand or in a food processor. When cooking, the secrets of success are to cook it in the largest pan available, and make sure the water is boiling when you add the pasta. Cook at a rolling boil, and don't overdrain it. Whatever you do, don't rinse the pasta and never overcook it as it will be soft and mushy—*al dente* (firm to the bite) is the best result. On that note, try these easy recipes and enjoy the delicious dishes they make.

Basic recipes

BASIC PASTA DOUGH

This is the most basic recipe for making pasta dough by hand or using a food processor. You can add colorings and flavorings according to the dish (see right).

SERVES 3–4

1⅓ cups white all-purpose flour or white
    bread flour, plus extra for dusting
pinch of salt
2 eggs, lightly beaten
1 tbsp olive oil

• To make the pasta dough by hand, sift the flour and salt onto a clean counter and make a well in the center. Pour the eggs and oil into the well, then using your fingers, gradually combine them and incorporate the flour.
• Turn out the dough onto a lightly floured counter and knead until smooth. Wrap the dough in plastic wrap and let rest for at least 30 minutes before rolling out or feeding through a pasta machine, as this makes it more elastic. Use as required.
• Alternatively, if you wish to use a food processor, sift the flour into the bowl of the food processor and add the salt.
• Pour in the eggs and olive oil, add any flavoring, and process until the dough begins to come together.
• Turn out the dough onto a lightly floured counter and knead until smooth. Wrap the dough in plastic wrap and let rest for at least 30 minutes before rolling out or feeding through a pasta machine, as this makes it more elastic. Use as required.

FLAVORED PASTA

TOMATO PASTA: Add 2 tablespoons tomato paste to the flour when making the dough and use 1½ eggs instead of 2.

HERB PASTA: Add 3 tablespoons chopped fresh herbs to the flour.

SPINACH PASTA: Squeeze out as much liquid as possible from 5½ oz/150 g thawed frozen spinach or 8 oz/225 g fresh spinach blanched in boiling water for 1 minute. Chop finely and mix thoroughly with the flour.

WHOLE WHEAT PASTA: Use a scant 1¼ cups whole wheat flour sifted with 3 tablespoons white all-purpose flour.

BÉCHAMEL SAUCE

MAKES 1¼ CUPS

1¼ cups milk
1 bay leaf
6 black peppercorns
slice of onion
mace blade
2 tbsp butter
3 tbsp all-purpose flour
salt and pepper

• Pour the milk into a pan and add the bay leaf, peppercorns, onion, and mace. Heat gently to just below boiling point, then remove from the heat, cover, and let infuse for 10 minutes. Strain the milk into a pitcher.
• Melt the butter in a separate pan. Sprinkle in the flour and cook over low heat, stirring constantly, for 1 minute. Remove from the heat and gradually stir in the milk. Return to the heat and bring to a boil, stirring. Cook, stirring, until thickened and smooth. Season to taste with salt and pepper.

With such a variety of shapes and sizes available, pasta is an extremely versatile food, which lends itself perfectly to many different dishes. It can be served hot or cold, and is not only perfect for main meals but can also be used in numerous delicious soups, appetizers, and light meals, as the recipes in this chapter illustrate.

Some types of pasta are specially designed for soups, as they cook in a short time. These include small rings of anellini, small shells of conchigliette, small butterflies of farfalline, and stars of stelline, along with many more. For children there are small shapes of the alphabet, known as alfabeto, which are always popular. Pasta soups are ideal for using up all those odds and ends of pasta that you have tucked away in the pantry, as in the recipe for White Bean Soup. Get them out now and use them up!

LIGHT FANTASTIC

In Italy, pasta is served as a first course, and although this may seem rather substantial to those not used to it, it is because servings are small and may be followed by a simple broiled fish or meat dish, without numerous accompaniments. Pasta also makes an ideal base for a salad for a perfect light lunch or supper dish. What could be more tempting on a summer's day than a Mediterranean-style salad of griddled fresh tuna steaks, spirals of pasta, green beans, and tomatoes, tossed in a lemony dressing, or pasta shells and charbroiled bell peppers tossed in pesto? It makes your mouth water just thinking about it!

SERVES 8

4 oz/115 g green beans
7 oz/200 g spinach leaves
8 oz/225 g plum tomatoes
2 onions, sliced
2 carrots, diced
2 celery stalks, sliced
2 potatoes, diced
1 cup frozen peas

2 zucchini, diced
3 garlic cloves, sliced
4 tbsp olive oil
8 cups vegetable or chicken stock
5 oz/140 g dried soup pasta
salt and pepper
freshly grated Parmesan cheese,
   to serve

PESTO

2 garlic cloves
¼ cup pine nuts
4 oz/115 g fresh basil leaves
½ cup freshly grated
   Parmesan cheese
½ cup olive oil
salt

Genoese Vegetable Soup

Any leftover pesto may be stored in a screw-top jar in the refrigerator for up to two weeks, or used as a sauce for pasta.

• Cut the green beans into 1-inch/2.5-cm lengths. Remove any coarse stalks from the spinach and shred. Peel the tomatoes by cutting a cross in the bottom of each and placing in a heatproof bowl. Cover with boiling water and let stand for 35–45 seconds. Drain and plunge into cold water, then the skins will slide off easily. Seed and dice the tomatoes, then place in a large, heavy-bottom pan together with the onions, carrots, celery, potatoes, peas, zucchini, and garlic. Pour in the olive oil and stock and bring to a boil over medium–low heat. Reduce the heat and let simmer gently for about 1½ hours.

• Meanwhile, make the Pesto. Put the garlic, pine nuts, basil, and a pinch of salt into a mortar and pound to a paste with a pestle. Transfer the mixture to a bowl and gradually work in the Parmesan cheese, using a wooden spoon, followed by the olive oil, to make a thick, creamy sauce. Taste and adjust the seasoning if necessary. Cover with plastic wrap and let chill in the refrigerator until required.

• Season the soup to taste with salt and pepper and add the pasta. Cook for an additional 8–10 minutes, or until the pasta is tender but still firm to the bite. The soup should be very thick. Stir in half the Pesto, remove the pan from the heat, and let stand for 4 minutes. Taste and adjust the seasoning, adding more salt, pepper, and Pesto if necessary. Ladle into warmed bowls and serve immediately. Hand round the grated Parmesan cheese separately.

SERVES 6

2 tbsp olive oil

2 oz/55 g rindless pancetta
or lean bacon, diced

2 onions, sliced

2 garlic cloves, finely chopped

3 carrots, chopped

2 celery stalks, chopped

1 cup dried cannellini beans, soaked
in cold water to cover overnight

14 oz/400 g canned chopped
tomatoes

8 cups beef stock

12 oz/350 g potatoes, diced

6 oz/175 g dried pepe bucato,
macaroni, or other soup pasta

6 oz/175 g green beans, sliced

1 cup fresh or frozen peas

8 oz/225 g savoy cabbage, shredded

3 tbsp chopped fresh flat-leaf parsley

salt and pepper

fresh Parmesan cheese shavings,
to serve

Minestrone Milanese

It usually takes
1½–2 hours of cooking
for soaked cannellini beans
to become tender, but this
can vary depending on how
long they have been stored.

• Heat the olive oil in a large, heavy-bottom pan. Add the pancetta, onions, and garlic and cook, stirring occasionally, for 5 minutes.

• Add the carrots and celery and cook, stirring occasionally, for an additional 5 minutes, or until all the vegetables are softened.

• Drain the soaked beans and add them to the pan with the tomatoes and their can juices and the beef stock. Bring to a boil, then reduce the heat, cover, and let simmer for 1 hour.

• Add the potatoes, re-cover, and cook for 15 minutes, then add the pasta, green beans, peas, cabbage, and parsley. Cover and cook for an additional 15 minutes, or until all the vegetables are tender. Season to taste with salt and pepper. Ladle the soup into warmed soup bowls and serve immediately with Parmesan cheese shavings.

SERVES 4

¾ cup dried cannellini beans, soaked
   in cold water to cover overnight
1½ quarts chicken or vegetable stock
4 oz/115 g dried corallini,
   conchigliette piccole,
   or other soup pasta

6 tbsp olive oil
2 garlic cloves, finely chopped
4 tbsp chopped fresh flat-leaf parsley
salt and pepper
fresh crusty bread, to serve

White Bean Soup

Beans feature widely in Tuscan cuisine. This smooth, comforting soup, in which beans are simmered for 2 hours, is very simple to make. Garlic and parsley, stirred in just before serving, complement the flavor, and a drizzle of olive oil adds the final touch.

• Drain the soaked beans and place them in a large, heavy-bottom pan. Add the stock and bring to a boil. Partially cover the pan, reduce the heat, and let simmer for 2 hours, or until tender.

• Transfer about half the beans and a little of the stock to a food processor or blender and process to a smooth purée. Return the purée to the pan and stir well to mix. Return the soup to a boil.

• Add the pasta to the soup, return to a boil, and cook for 10 minutes, or until tender.

• Meanwhile, heat 4 tablespoons of the olive oil in a small pan. Add the garlic and cook over low heat, stirring frequently, for 4–5 minutes, or until golden. Stir the garlic into the soup and add the parsley. Season to taste with salt and pepper and ladle into warmed soup bowls. Drizzle with the remaining olive oil and serve immediately with crusty bread.

SERVES 4

12 oz/350 g dried ziti, broken into
   1½-inch/ 4-cm lengths
5 tbsp extra virgin olive oil
2 garlic cloves, lightly crushed
7 oz/200 g arugula

2 fresh red chilies, thickly sliced
salt
fresh red chili flowers, to garnish
freshly grated romano cheese,
   to serve

Ziti with Arugula

Wild arugula has a more pungent, peppery flavor than the cultivated variety. However, if you find that it is too strong, blanch the leaves for 1 minute in boiling water and pat dry before stir-frying.

• Bring a large, heavy-bottom pan of lightly salted water to a boil. Add the pasta, return to a boil, and cook for 8–10 minutes, or until tender but still firm to the bite.

• Meanwhile, heat the olive oil in a large, heavy-bottom skillet. Add the garlic, arugula, and chilies and stir-fry for 5 minutes, or until the arugula has wilted.

• Stir 2 tablespoons of the pasta cooking water into the arugula, then drain the pasta and add to the skillet. Cook, stirring frequently, for 2 minutes, then transfer to a warmed serving dish. Remove and discard the garlic cloves and chilies, garnish with red chili flowers, and serve immediately with the romano cheese.

SERVES 4
1 lb/450 g dried farfalle
2 tbsp unsalted butter
3 cups baby peas
generous ¾ cup heavy cream
pinch of freshly grated nutmeg

salt and pepper
fresh flat-leaf parsley sprigs,
    to garnish
½ cup freshly grated Parmesan
    cheese, plus extra to serve
crusty bread, to serve

Farfalle with Cream and Parmesan

This dish is traditionally named fettucine Alfredo and is made without the baby peas. Adding the baby peas creates a more substantial meal.

• Bring a large pan of lightly salted water to a boil. Add the pasta, return to a boil, and cook for 8–10 minutes, or until tender but still firm to the bite, then drain thoroughly.

• Melt the butter in a large, heavy-bottom pan. Add the baby peas and cook for 2–3 minutes. Add ⅔ cup of the cream and bring to a boil. Reduce the heat and simmer for 1 minute, or until slightly thickened.

• Add the drained pasta to the cream mixture. Place the pan over low heat and toss until the farfalle are thoroughly coated. Season to taste with nutmeg, salt, and pepper, then add the remaining cream and the grated Parmesan cheese. Toss again and transfer to individual serving bowls. Garnish with parsley sprigs and serve immediately with extra Parmesan cheese for sprinkling and crusty bread.

SERVES 4

2 tbsp lemon juice

4 baby globe artichokes

7 tbsp olive oil

2 shallots, finely chopped

2 garlic cloves, finely chopped

2 tbsp chopped fresh flat-leaf parsley

2 tbsp chopped fresh mint

12 oz/350 g dried rigatoni
or other tubular pasta

12 large raw shrimp

2 tbsp unsalted butter

salt and pepper

Springtime Pasta

Look for globe artichokes that have tightly packed, deep green leaves with a minimum of browning, and those that are heavy relative to their size.

• Fill a large bowl with cold water and add the lemon juice. Prepare the artichokes one at a time. Cut off the stems and trim away any tough outer leaves. Cut across the tops of the leaves. Slice in half lengthwise and remove the central fibrous chokes, then cut lengthwise into 1/4-inch/ 5-mm thick slices. Immediately place the slices in the bowl of acidulated water to prevent discoloration.

• Heat 5 tablespoons of the olive oil in a heavy-bottom skillet. Drain the artichoke slices and pat dry with paper towels. Add them to the skillet with the shallots, garlic, parsley, and mint and cook over low heat, stirring frequently, for 10–12 minutes, or until tender.

• Meanwhile, bring a large pan of lightly salted water to a boil. Add the pasta, return to a boil, and cook for 8–10 minutes, or until tender but still firm to the bite.

• Shell the shrimp, cut a slit along the back of each, and remove and discard the dark vein. Melt the butter in a small skillet, cut the shrimp in half, and add them to the skillet. Cook, stirring occasionally, for 2–3 minutes, or until the shrimp have changed color. Season to taste with salt and pepper.

• Drain the pasta and tip it into a bowl. Add the remaining olive oil and toss well. Add the artichoke mixture and the shrimp and toss again. Serve immediately.

SERVES 4

12 oz/350 g dried bavettine

2 tbsp olive oil

1 garlic clove, finely chopped

4 oz/115 g smoked salmon,
    cut into thin strips

2 oz/55 g arugula

salt and pepper

½ lemon, to garnish

Bavettine with Smoked Salmon and Arugula

Do not overcook the salmon or arugula; they should just be warmed through and the arugula lightly wilted. If arugula is unavailable, use baby spinach leaves instead.

• Bring a large, heavy-bottom pan of lightly salted water to a boil. Add the pasta, return to a boil, and cook for 8–10 minutes, or until tender but still firm to the bite.

• Just before the end of the cooking time, heat the olive oil in a heavy-bottom skillet. Add the garlic and cook over low heat, stirring constantly, for 1 minute. Do not allow the garlic to brown or it will taste bitter. Add the salmon and arugula. Season to taste with salt and pepper and cook, stirring constantly, for 1 minute. Remove the skillet from the heat.

• Drain the pasta and transfer to a warmed serving dish. Add the smoked salmon and arugula mixture, toss lightly, and serve, garnished with a lemon half.

SERVES 4

4 oz/115 g green beans, cut into 2-inch/5-cm lengths

8 oz/225 g dried fusilli tricolore

generous ⅓ cup olive oil

2 tuna steaks, about 12 oz/350 g each

6 cherry tomatoes, halved

⅓ cup black olives, pitted and halved

6 canned anchovies, drained and chopped

3 tbsp chopped fresh flat-leaf parsley

2 tbsp lemon juice

8–10 radicchio leaves

salt and pepper

Pasta Niçoise

Brushing or spraying the grill pan with oil helps prevent the food sticking. After cooking, let the grill pan cool. Do not plunge it into cold water, as this may warp the pan.

• Bring a large, heavy-bottom pan of lightly salted water to a boil. Add the green beans, reduce the heat, and cook for 5–6 minutes. Remove with a slotted spoon and refresh in a bowl of cold water. Drain well. Add the pasta to the same pan, return to a boil, and cook for 8–10 minutes, or until tender but still firm to the bite.

• Meanwhile, brush a grill pan with some of the olive oil and heat until smoking. Season the tuna to taste with salt and pepper and brush both sides with some of the remaining olive oil. Cook over medium heat for 2 minutes on each side, or until cooked to your liking, then remove from the grill pan and reserve.

• Drain the pasta well and tip it into a bowl. Add the green beans, cherry tomatoes, olives, anchovies, parsley, lemon juice, and remaining olive oil and season to taste with salt and pepper. Toss well and let cool. Remove and discard any skin from the tuna and slice thickly.

• Gently mix the tuna into the pasta salad. Line a large salad bowl with the radicchio leaves, spoon in the salad, and serve.

SERVES 4

1 red bell pepper

1 orange bell pepper

10 oz/280 g dried conchiglie (pasta
shells)

5 tbsp extra virgin olive oil

2 tbsp lemon juice

2 tbsp pesto

1 garlic clove, very finely chopped

3 tbsp shredded fresh basil leaves

salt and pepper

Pasta Salad with Bell Peppers

This salad can be made very easily without the pasta. When the bell peppers have been under the broiler for 10 minutes, add 4 tomatoes and broil for an additional 5 minutes. Cover the bell peppers with paper towels, then peel and chop as described in the recipe. Peel and coarsely chop the tomatoes. Combine them with the pesto dressing and garnish with black olives.

• Put the whole bell peppers on a baking sheet and place under a preheated broiler, turning frequently, for 15 minutes, until charred all over. Remove with tongs and place in a bowl. Cover with crumpled paper towels and set aside.

• Meanwhile, bring a large pan of lightly salted water to a boil. Add the pasta, bring back to a boil, and cook for 8–10 minutes, until tender but still firm to the bite.

• Combine the olive oil, lemon juice, pesto, and garlic in a bowl, whisking well to mix. Drain the pasta, add it to the pesto mixture while still hot, and toss well. Set aside.

• When the bell peppers are cool enough to handle, peel off the skins, then cut open and remove the seeds. Chop the flesh coarsely and add to the pasta with the basil. Season to taste with salt and pepper and toss well. Serve at room temperature.

SERVES 4

8 oz/225 g dried farfalle or other
    pasta shapes
6 pieces of sun-dried tomato in oil,
    drained and chopped
4 scallions, chopped

2 oz/55 g arugula, shredded
½ cucumber, seeded and diced
2 tbsp freshly grated
    Parmesan cheese
salt and pepper

DRESSING

4 tbsp olive oil
½ tsp superfine sugar
1 tbsp white wine vinegar
1 tsp Dijon mustard
4 fresh basil leaves, finely shredded
salt and pepper

Warm Pasta Salad

It makes it easier to toss the pasta if you use 2 forks or 2 tablespoons, and before adding the dressing to the salad, whisk it again until emulsified. Add the dressing just before serving.

• To make the dressing, whisk the olive oil, sugar, vinegar, and mustard together in a bowl. Season to taste with salt and pepper. Stir in the basil.

• Bring a large, heavy-bottom pan of lightly salted water to a boil. Add the pasta, return to a boil, and cook for 8–10 minutes, or until tender but still firm to the bite. Drain and transfer to a salad bowl. Add the dressing and toss well.

• Add the chopped sun-dried tomatoes, scallions, arugula, and cucumber, season to taste with salt and pepper, and toss. Sprinkle with the Parmesan cheese and serve warm.

There is a vast choice of sauces to dress pasta, from the simplest pesto or Olio e Aglio, to Pumpkin or Chicken and Porcini. Of all the pasta dishes in the country, spaghetti with meatballs is probably the most loved. However, it isn't an authentic Italian dish at all—in Italy they would never serve so much meat with their pasta. When it comes to choosing a variety of pasta to serve with a particular sauce, suggestions are given in the recipes, but should you wish to use another shape, although there are no hard-and-fast rules, there is a general rule of thumb. Long, thin pastas are ideal for simple sauces such as Pesto, while thicker strands are good with a meat, fish, cheese, cream, mushroom, or smooth tomato sauce. Short, tubular pasta, twists, and shells, which have hollows and cavities for the sauce to cling to, go well with thicker, chunkier sauces.

SIMPLE SAUCES

What is important is that the pasta isn't drowned in the sauce. There should be just enough sauce to coat it lightly and not leave a pool on the plate once the pasta has been eaten. Finally, don't overlook the quickest pasta sauce that you can make—melted butter or olive oil with plenty of freshly ground black pepper and perhaps a handful of chopped fresh herbs. It is often the simple things in life that are the best!

SERVES 4

2 tbsp olive oil

1 tbsp butter

1 small onion, finely chopped

1 carrot, finely chopped

1 celery stalk, finely chopped

1¾ oz/50 g mushrooms, diced

8 oz/225 g ground beef

2¾ oz/75 g unsmoked bacon
or ham, diced

2 chicken livers, chopped

2 tbsp tomato paste

½ cup dry white wine

½ tsp freshly grated nutmeg

1¼ cups chicken stock

½ cup heavy cream

1 lb/450 g dried spaghetti

salt and pepper

2 tbsp chopped fresh flat-leaf parsley,
to garnish

freshly grated Parmesan, to serve

Spaghetti Bolognese

This classic meat sauce (ragù) from Bologna can also be made with ground veal or half beef and half pork, and the cream can be omitted. If you choose to omit it, and the sauce becomes too dry, add a little warm water.

• Heat the olive oil and butter in a large pan over medium heat. Add the onion, carrot, celery, and mushrooms to the pan, then cook until soft. Add the beef and bacon and cook until the beef is evenly browned.

• Stir in the chicken livers and tomato paste and cook for 2–3 minutes. Pour in the wine and season with salt, pepper, and the nutmeg. Add the stock. Bring to a boil, then cover and simmer gently over low heat for 1 hour. Stir in the cream and simmer, uncovered, until reduced.

• Bring a large pan of lightly salted water to a boil. Add the pasta, return to a boil, and cook until tender but still firm to the bite. Drain and transfer to a warmed serving dish.

• Pour half the sauce over the pasta. Toss well. Spoon the meat sauce over the pasta, garnish with parsley, and serve with Parmesan cheese.

SERVES 4

3 tbsp olive oil

1 onion, chopped

1 red bell pepper, seeded and diced

1 orange bell pepper, seeded
     and diced

1 lb 12 oz/800 g canned
     chopped tomatoes

1 tbsp sun-dried tomato paste

1 tsp paprika

8 oz/225 g pepperoni, sliced

2 tbsp chopped fresh flat-leaf parsley,
     plus extra to garnish

1 lb/450 g dried garganelli

salt and pepper

mixed salad greens, to serve

Pepperoni Pasta

Pepperoni is a hotly spiced Italian sausage made from pork and beef and flavored with fennel. You could substitute other spicy sausages, such as kabanos or chorizo, if you like. If you cannot find garganelli pasta, then use penne or another pasta shape, such as fusilli, bucati, or farfalle.

• Heat 2 tablespoons of the olive oil in a large, heavy-bottom skillet. Add the onion and cook over low heat, stirring occasionally, for 5 minutes, or until softened. Add the red and orange bell peppers, tomatoes and their can juices, sun-dried tomato paste, and paprika to the pan and bring to a boil.

• Add the pepperoni and parsley and season to taste with salt and pepper. Stir well and bring to a boil, then reduce the heat and simmer for 10–15 minutes.

• Meanwhile, bring a large, heavy-bottom pan of lightly salted water to a boil. Add the pasta, return to a boil, and cook for 8–10 minutes, or until tender but still firm to the bite. Drain well and transfer to a warmed serving dish. Add the remaining olive oil and toss. Add the sauce and toss again. Sprinkle with parsley and serve immediately with mixed salad greens.

SERVES 6
1 potato, diced
14 oz/400 g ground steak
1 onion, finely chopped
1 egg
4 tbsp chopped fresh flat-leaf parsley

all-purpose flour, for dusting
5 tbsp virgin olive oil
1¾ cups strained canned tomatoes
2 tbsp tomato paste
14 oz/400 g dried spaghetti
salt and pepper

TO GARNISH
6 fresh basil leaves, shredded
freshly grated Parmesan cheese

Spaghetti with Meatballs

The humble meatball, served Italian-American style over spaghetti or tagliatelle, is elevated here to greater heights by using fresh ground steak. The meatballs are tender and succulent and enjoyed by both children and adults alike.

• Place the potato in a small pan, add cold water to cover and a pinch of salt, and bring to a boil. Cook for 10–15 minutes until tender, then drain. Either mash thoroughly with a potato masher or fork or pass through a potato ricer.

• Combine the potato, steak, onion, egg, and parsley in a bowl and season to taste with salt and pepper. Spread out the flour on a plate. With dampened hands, shape the meat mixture into walnut-size balls and roll in the flour. Shake off any excess.

• Heat the olive oil in a heavy-bottom skillet, add the meatballs, and cook over medium heat, stirring and turning frequently, for 8–10 minutes, or until golden all over.

• Add the strained tomatoes and tomato paste and cook for an additional 10 minutes, or until the sauce is reduced and thickened.

• Meanwhile, bring a large pan of lightly salted water to a boil. Add the pasta, return to a boil, and cook for 8–10 minutes, or until tender but still firm to the bite.

• Drain well and add to the meatball sauce, tossing well to coat. Transfer to a warmed serving dish, garnish with the basil leaves and grated Parmesan cheese, and serve immediately.

SERVES 4

1½ oz/40 g dried porcini mushrooms

¾ cup hot water

1 lb 12 oz/800 g canned
    chopped tomatoes

1 fresh red chili, seeded
    and finely chopped

3 tbsp olive oil

12 oz/350 g skinless, boneless
    chicken, cut into thin strips

2 garlic cloves, finely chopped

12 oz/350 g dried pappardelle

salt and pepper

2 tbsp chopped fresh flat-leaf parsley,
    to garnish

Pappardelle with Chicken and Porcini

Wild mushrooms are used extensively in Italian dishes and porcini mushrooms are the most popular. When using porcini, always soak them first in hot water for 30 minutes, then drain well before cooking.

• Place the porcini in a small bowl, add the hot water, and let soak for 30 minutes. Meanwhile, place the tomatoes and their can juices in a heavy-bottom pan and break them up with a wooden spoon, then stir in the chili. Bring to a boil, then reduce the heat and simmer, stirring occasionally, for 30 minutes, or until reduced.

• Remove the mushrooms from their soaking liquid with a slotted spoon, reserving the liquid. Strain the liquid through a coffee filter paper or cheesecloth-lined strainer into the tomatoes and simmer for an additional 15 minutes. Meanwhile, heat 2 tablespoons of the olive oil in a heavy-bottom skillet. Add the chicken and cook, stirring frequently, until golden brown all over and tender. Stir in the mushrooms and garlic and cook for an additional 5 minutes.

• While the chicken is cooking, bring a large, heavy-bottom pan of lightly salted water to a boil. Add the pasta, return to a boil, and cook for 8–10 minutes, or until tender but still firm to the bite. Drain well, then transfer to a warmed serving dish. Drizzle the pasta with the remaining olive oil and toss lightly. Stir the chicken mixture into the tomato sauce, season to taste with salt and pepper, and spoon onto the pasta. Toss lightly, sprinkle with parsley, and serve immediately.

SERVES 4

1 lb/450 g dried spaghetti

1 tbsp olive oil

8 oz/225 g rindless pancetta
or lean bacon, chopped

4 eggs

5 tbsp light cream

4 tbsp freshly grated
Parmesan cheese

salt and pepper

Spaghetti alla Carbonara

For a more substantial dish, cook 1–2 finely chopped shallots with the pancetta and add 4 oz/115 g sliced mushrooms after 4 minutes, then continue as above.

• Bring a large, heavy-bottom pan of lightly salted water to a boil. Add the pasta, return to a boil, and cook for 8–10 minutes, or until tender but still firm to the bite.

• Meanwhile, heat the olive oil in a heavy-bottom skillet. Add the chopped pancetta and cook over medium heat, stirring frequently, for 8–10 minutes.

• Beat the eggs with the cream in a small bowl and season to taste with salt and pepper. Drain the pasta and return it to the pan. Tip in the contents of the skillet, then add the egg mixture and half the Parmesan cheese. Stir well, then transfer to a warmed serving dish. Serve immediately, sprinkled with the remaining Parmesan cheese.

SERVES 4

1 lb/450 g plum tomatoes

3 tbsp olive oil

2 garlic cloves, finely chopped

10 anchovy fillets, drained
and chopped

¾ cup black olives, pitted
and chopped

1 tbsp capers, rinsed

pinch of cayenne pepper

14 oz/400 g dried linguine

salt

2 tbsp chopped fresh flat-leaf
parsley, to garnish

Linguine alla Puttanesca

Salted anchovies have a much better flavor than canned fillets, but are not so widely available. If you can find them, soak them in cold water for 30 minutes, then pat dry with paper towels before using.

• Peel the tomatoes by cutting a cross in the bottom of each and placing in a heatproof bowl. Cover with boiling water and let stand for 35–45 seconds. Drain and plunge into cold water, then the skins will slide off easily. Seed and chop the tomatoes.

• Heat the olive oil in a heavy-bottom pan. Add the garlic and cook over low heat, stirring frequently, for 2 minutes. Add the anchovies and mash them to a pulp with a fork. Add the olives, capers, and tomatoes and season to taste with cayenne pepper. Cover and let simmer for 25 minutes.

• Meanwhile, bring a pan of lightly salted water to a boil. Add the pasta, return to a boil, and cook for 8–10 minutes, or until tender but still firm to the bite. Drain and transfer to a warmed serving dish.

• Spoon the anchovy sauce into the dish and toss the pasta, using 2 large forks. Garnish with the parsley and serve immediately.

SERVES 4

2 lb 4 oz/1 kg live clams

¾ cup water

¾ cup dry white wine

12 oz/350 g dried spaghetti

5 tbsp olive oil

2 garlic cloves, finely chopped

4 tbsp chopped fresh flat-leaf parsley

salt and pepper

Spaghetti with Clams

In Italy, this dish would be prepared with small, smooth-shelled clams, known as vongole, but you can use other varieties, such as cherrystone clams. If fresh clams are not available, substitute with 10 oz/280 g of clams in brine, which are sold in jars.

• Scrub the clams under cold running water and discard any with broken or damaged shells and any that do not shut when sharply tapped. Place the clams in a large, heavy-bottom pan, add the water and wine, cover, and cook over high heat, shaking the pan occasionally, for 5 minutes, or until the shells have opened.

• Remove the clams with a slotted spoon and let cool slightly. Strain the cooking liquid through a cheesecloth-lined strainer into a small pan. Bring to a boil and cook until reduced by about half, then remove from the heat. Meanwhile, discard any clams that have not opened, remove the remainder from their shells, and reserve until required.

• Bring a large pan of lightly salted water to a boil. Add the pasta, return to a boil, and cook for 8–10 minutes, or until tender but still firm to the bite.

• Meanwhile, heat the olive oil in a large, heavy-bottom skillet. Add the garlic and cook, stirring frequently, for 2 minutes. Add the parsley and the reduced clam cooking liquid and let simmer gently.

• Drain the pasta and add it to the skillet with the clams. Season to taste with salt and pepper and cook, stirring constantly, for 4 minutes, or until the pasta is coated and the clams have heated through. Transfer to a warmed serving dish and serve immediately.

SERVES 4

1 lb/450 g dried tagliatelle

salt

fresh basil sprigs, to garnish

PESTO

2 garlic cloves

¼ cup pine nuts

4 oz/115 g fresh basil leaves

½ cup freshly grated
   Parmesan cheese

½ cup olive oil

salt

Pasta with Pesto

For different flavor variations, try using fresh mint, oregano, or even cilantro in place of the fresh basil leaves in the pesto.

• To make the pesto, put the garlic, pine nuts, a large pinch of salt, and the basil into a mortar and pound to a paste with a pestle. Transfer to a bowl and gradually work in the Parmesan cheese with a wooden spoon, followed by the olive oil, to make a thick, creamy sauce. Taste and adjust the seasoning if necessary.

• Alternatively, put the garlic, pine nuts, and a large pinch of salt into a food processor or blender and process briefly. Add the basil leaves and process to a paste. With the motor still running, gradually add the olive oil. Scrape into a bowl and beat in the Parmesan cheese. Season to taste with salt.

• Bring a large pan of lightly salted water to a boil. Add the pasta, return to a boil, and cook for 8–10 minutes, or until tender but still firm to the bite. Drain the pasta well, return to the pan, and toss with half the pesto, then divide among warmed serving plates and top with the remaining pesto. Garnish the pasta with basil sprigs and serve immediately.

SERVES 4

1 lb/450 g dried spaghetti

½ cup extra virgin olive oil

3 garlic cloves, finely chopped

3 tbsp chopped fresh flat-leaf parsley

salt and pepper

Spaghetti Olio e Aglio

Cooked pasta gets cold quickly, so make sure that the serving dish is warmed thoroughly and as soon as the pasta is drained, transfer to the dish.

• Bring a large, heavy-bottom pan of lightly salted water to a boil. Add the spaghetti, return to a boil, and cook for 8–10 minutes, or until tender but still firm to the bite.

• Meanwhile, heat the olive oil in a heavy-bottom skillet. Add the garlic and a pinch of salt and cook over low heat, stirring constantly, for 3–4 minutes, or until golden. Do not allow the garlic to brown or it will taste bitter. Remove the skillet from the heat.

• Drain the pasta and transfer to a warmed serving dish. Pour in the garlic-flavored olive oil, then add the chopped parsley and season to taste with salt and pepper. Toss well and serve immediately.

SERVES 4

4 tbsp butter

1 tbsp olive oil

6 shallots, sliced

1 lb/450 g cremini mushrooms,
    sliced

salt and pepper

1 tsp all-purpose flour

2/3 cup heavy cream or
    panna da cucina

2 tbsp port

4 oz/115 g sun-dried tomatoes in oil,
    drained and chopped

pinch of freshly grated nutmeg

12 oz/350 g dried penne

2 tbsp chopped fresh flatleaf parsley

Penne with Creamy Mushrooms

Nutmeg is used widely in Italian cooking as it has a fragrant, sweet aroma. Use freshly grated nutmeg rather than ground, which rapidly deteriorates. Store it in an airtight container.

• Melt the butter with the olive oil in a large heavy-bottom skillet. Add the shallots and cook over low heat, stirring occasionally, for 4–5 minutes, or until softened. Add the mushrooms and cook for an additional 2 minutes. Season to taste with salt and pepper, then sprinkle in the flour and cook, stirring, for 1 minute.

• Remove the skillet from the heat and gradually stir in the cream and port. Return to the heat, add the sun-dried tomatoes and grated nutmeg, and cook over low heat, stirring occasionally, for 8 minutes.

• Meanwhile, bring a large heavy-bottom pan of lightly salted water to a boil. Add the pasta, return to a boil, and cook for 8–10 minutes, or until tender but still firm to the bite. Drain well and add to the mushroom sauce. Cook for 3 minutes, then transfer to a warmed serving dish. Sprinkle with the chopped parsley and serve immediately.

SERVES 4

12 oz/350 g dried fusilli

3 tbsp olive oil

12 oz/350 g wild mushrooms
    or white mushrooms, sliced

1 garlic clove, finely chopped

1¾ cups heavy cream

9 oz/250 g Gorgonzola cheese,
    crumbled

salt and pepper

2 tbsp chopped fresh flat-leaf parsley,
    to garnish

Fusilli with Gorgonzola and Mushroom Sauce

Wild mushrooms have a much earthier flavor than cultivated ones, so they complement the strong taste of the cheese. Porcini are especially delicious, but rather expensive. Portobello mushrooms would also be a good choice. Otherwise, use cultivated mushrooms, but add 1 oz/25 g dried porcini, soaked for 30 minutes in 1 cup hot water.

• Bring a large pan of lightly salted water to a boil. Add the pasta, return to a boil, and cook for 8–10 minutes, or until tender but still firm to the bite.

• Meanwhile, heat the olive oil in a heavy-bottom pan. Add the mushrooms and cook over low heat, stirring frequently, for 5 minutes. Add the garlic and cook for an additional 2 minutes.

• Add the cream, bring to a boil, and cook for 1 minute until slightly thickened. Stir in the cheese and cook over low heat until it has melted. Do not allow the sauce to boil once the cheese has been added. Season to taste with salt and pepper and remove the pan from the heat.

• Drain the pasta and tip it into the sauce. Toss well to coat, then serve immediately, garnished with the parsley.

SERVES 4

2/3 cup dry white wine

1 tbsp sun-dried tomato paste

2 fresh red chilies

2 garlic cloves, finely chopped

12 oz/350 g dried tortiglioni

4 tbsp chopped fresh flat-leaf parsley

salt and pepper

fresh romano cheese shavings,
  to garnish

SUGOCASA

5 tbsp extra virgin olive oil

1 lb/450 g plum tomatoes, chopped

salt and pepper

Hot Chili Pasta

If time is short, use ready-made sugocasa, which is available from specialty stores, sometimes labeled "crushed tomatoes." You could also use strained canned tomatoes, but the sauce will be thinner.

• First make the sugocasa. Heat the olive oil in a skillet until it is almost smoking. Add the tomatoes and cook over high heat for 2–3 minutes. Reduce the heat to low and cook gently for 20 minutes, or until very soft. Season with salt and pepper, then pass through a food mill or blender into a clean pan.

• Add the wine, sun-dried tomato paste, whole chilies, and garlic to the sugocasa and bring to a boil. Reduce the heat and simmer gently.

• Meanwhile, bring a large pan of lightly salted water to a boil. Add the pasta, return to a boil, and cook for 8–10 minutes, or until tender but still firm to the bite.

• Meanwhile, remove the chilies and taste the sauce. If you prefer a hotter flavor, chop some or all of the chilies and return them to the pan. Check the seasoning at the same time, then stir in half the parsley.

• Drain the pasta and tip it into a warmed serving bowl. Add the sauce and toss to coat. Sprinkle with the remaining parsley, garnish with the romano shavings, and serve immediately.

The majority of baked pasta dishes, the two most well known perhaps being lasagna and macaroni and cheese, have one thing in common, which is that the ingredients are prepared or cooked separately and then assembled in the dish just before baking in the oven. Pasta, other ingredients such as meat, cheese, or vegetables, and a sauce are the typical components. One part of these dishes that you will need time and time again is Béchamel Sauce and so it has been included on page 6 for easy reference.

The Italians even have a name for these baked dishes—it is called pasticci. Many baked pasta dishes are traditional dishes, since pasticci were often served at banquets as far back as the eighteenth century. In those days they were known as timballi, but today the word timballo is used to describe a baked dish that is served turned out of its dish.

BAKED TO PERFECTION

These baked pasta dishes are substantial and are therefore suitable for serving as a main meal. They are also ideal for buffet parties when feeding a large number of people, as they are easy to serve and can be eaten with just a fork. An additional advantage is that they can be prepared in advance. All that is needed to accompany them is a fresh green salad.

SERVES 4

3 tbsp olive oil

1 onion, finely chopped

1 celery stalk, finely chopped

1 carrot, finely chopped

3½ oz/100 g pancetta or rindless lean bacon, finely chopped

6 oz/175 g ground beef

6 oz/175 g ground pork

generous ⅓ cup dry red wine

⅔ cup beef stock

1 tbsp tomato paste

1 clove

1 bay leaf

⅔ cup boiling milk

14 oz/400 g dried lasagna

4 tbsp unsalted butter, diced, plus extra for greasing

1¼ cups Béchamel Sauce

5 oz/140 g mozzarella cheese, diced

1¼ cups freshly grated Parmesan cheese

salt and pepper

Baked Lasagna

This classic Italian dish is a specialty of the Emilia-Romagna region, the gastronomic center of Italy. It can be made with dried or fresh lasagna and either verde (spinach) or egg lasagna. You could also use all ground beef or all ground pork if wished.

• Heat the olive oil in a large, heavy-bottom pan. Add the onion, celery, carrot, pancetta, beef, and pork and cook over medium heat, stirring frequently and breaking up the meat with a wooden spoon, for 10 minutes, or until lightly browned.

• Add the wine, bring to a boil, and cook until reduced. Add about two-thirds of the stock, bring to a boil, and cook until reduced. Combine the remaining stock and tomato paste and add to the pan. Season to taste with salt and pepper, add the clove and bay leaf, and pour in the milk. Cover and let simmer over a low heat for 1½ hours.

• Preheat the oven to 400°F/200°C. Unless you are using lasagna that needs no precooking, bring a large, heavy-bottom pan of lightly salted water to a boil. Add the lasagna sheets, in batches, return to a boil, and cook for about 10 minutes, or until tender but still firm to the bite. Remove with tongs and spread out on a clean dish towel. Remove the meat sauce from the heat and discard the clove and bay leaf.

• Lightly grease a large, ovenproof dish with butter. Place a layer of lasagna in the bottom and cover it with a layer of meat sauce. Spoon a layer of Béchamel Sauce on top and sprinkle with one-third of the mozzarella and Parmesan cheeses. Continue making layers until all the ingredients are used, ending with a topping of Béchamel Sauce and sprinkled cheese.

• Dot the top of the lasagna with the diced butter and bake in the preheated oven for 30 minutes, or until golden and bubbling.

SERVES 4

2 tbsp olive oil

1 onion, chopped

1 garlic clove, finely chopped

2 carrots, diced

2 oz/55 g pancetta or rindless
    lean bacon, chopped

4 oz/115 g mushrooms, chopped

1 lb/450 g ground pork

½ cup dry white wine

4 tbsp strained canned tomatoes

7 oz/200 g canned chopped tomatoes

2 tsp chopped fresh sage
    or ½ tsp dried sage

8 oz/225 g dried elicoidali

5 oz/140 g mozzarella cheese, diced

4 tbsp freshly grated
    Parmesan cheese

1¼ cups hot Béchamel Sauce

salt and pepper

Pork and Pasta Bake

When cooking with olive oil, there is no need to use extra virgin olive oil as the flavor will be lost during cooking. Olive oil is best stored in a cool place, out of direct sunlight. Do not store in the refrigerator.

• Preheat the oven to 400°F/200°C. Heat the olive oil in a large, heavy-bottom skillet. Add the onion, garlic, and carrots and cook over low heat, stirring occasionally, for 5 minutes, or until the onion has softened. Add the pancetta and cook for 5 minutes. Add the chopped mushrooms and cook, stirring occasionally, for an additional 2 minutes. Add the pork and cook, breaking it up with a wooden spoon, until the meat is browned all over. Stir in the wine, strained tomatoes, chopped tomatoes and their can juices, and sage. Season to taste with salt and pepper and bring to a boil, then cover and simmer over low heat for 25–30 minutes.

• Meanwhile, bring a large, heavy-bottom pan of lightly salted water to a boil. Add the pasta, return to a boil, and cook for 8–10 minutes, or until tender but still firm to the bite.

• Spoon the pork mixture into a large ovenproof dish. Stir the mozzarella and half the Parmesan cheese into the Béchamel Sauce. Drain the pasta and stir the sauce into it, then spoon it over the pork mixture. Sprinkle with the remaining Parmesan cheese and bake in the oven for 25–30 minutes, or until golden brown. Serve immediately.

SERVES 6

1/3 cup butter, plus extra for greasing

12 oz/350 g dried spaghetti

7 oz/200 g smoked salmon,
    cut into strips

10 oz/280 g jumbo shrimp, cooked,
    shelled, and deveined

1¼ cups Béchamel Sauce

1 cup freshly grated
    Parmesan cheese

salt

Layered Spaghetti with Smoked Salmon and Shrimp

This dish would also be delicious made with smoked halibut instead of the salmon and smoked mussels instead of the shrimp.

• Preheat the oven to 350°F/180°C. Grease a large ovenproof dish and reserve.

• Bring a large pan of lightly salted water to a boil. Add the pasta, return to a boil, and cook for 8–10 minutes, or until tender but still firm to the bite. Drain well, return to the pan, add 4 tablespoons of the butter, and toss well.

• Spoon half the spaghetti into the prepared dish, cover with the strips of smoked salmon, then top with the shrimp. Pour over half the Béchamel Sauce and sprinkle with half the Parmesan. Add the remaining spaghetti, cover with the remaining sauce, and sprinkle with the remaining Parmesan. Dice the remaining butter and dot it over the surface.

• Bake in the preheated oven for 15 minutes, or until the top is golden. Serve immediately.

SERVES 4

12 oz/350 g dried short-cut macaroni

6 tbsp butter, plus extra for greasing

2 small fennel bulbs, thinly sliced

6 oz/175 g mushrooms, thinly sliced

6 oz/175 g cooked shelled shrimp

pinch of cayenne pepper

1¼ cups Béchamel Sauce

½ cup freshly grated
   Parmesan cheese

2 large tomatoes, sliced

olive oil, for brushing

1 tsp dried oregano

salt and pepper

Macaroni and Seafood Bake

Fennel imparts a delicate anise flavor to dishes and goes very well with fish. To prepare the fennel bulbs, cut off the stalk and root end, then slice the bulbs lengthwise.

• Preheat the oven to 350°F/180°C. Bring a large pan of lightly salted water to a boil. Add the pasta, return to a boil, and cook for 8–10 minutes, or until tender but still firm to the bite. Drain and return to the pan. Add 2 tablespoons of the butter to the pasta, cover, shake the pan, and keep warm.

• Melt the remaining butter in a separate pan. Add the fennel and cook for 3–4 minutes. Stir in the mushrooms and cook for an additional 2 minutes. Stir in the shrimp, then remove the pan from the heat.

• Stir the cayenne pepper into the Béchamel Sauce and add the shrimp mixture and pasta.

• Grease a large ovenproof dish with butter, then pour the mixture into the dish and spread evenly. Sprinkle over the Parmesan cheese and arrange the tomato slices in a ring around the edge. Brush the tomatoes with olive oil, then sprinkle over the oregano. Bake in the preheated oven for 25 minutes, or until golden brown. Serve immediately.

SERVES 6

12 oz/350 g dried conchiglie

6 tbsp butter, plus extra for greasing

2 fennel bulbs, thinly sliced

6 oz/175 g mushrooms, thinly sliced

6 oz/175 g cooked shelled shrimp

6 oz/175 g cooked crabmeat

pinch of cayenne pepper

1¼ cups Béchamel Sauce

½ cup freshly grated
  Parmesan cheese

2 beefsteak tomatoes, sliced

olive oil, for brushing

salt

TO SERVE

green salad

crusty bread

Shellfish Bake

You can either use cooked fresh crabmeat or canned. If you wish to use fresh crab and time is limited, buy a ready-dressed crab.

• Preheat the oven to 350°F/180°C. Bring a large, heavy-bottom pan of lightly salted water to a boil. Add the pasta, return to a boil, and cook for 8–10 minutes, or until tender but still firm to the bite. Drain well, return to the pan, and stir in 2 tablespoons of the butter. Cover the pan and keep warm.

• Meanwhile, melt the remaining butter in a large, heavy-bottom skillet. Add the fennel and cook over medium heat for 5 minutes, or until softened. Stir in the mushrooms and cook for an additional 2 minutes. Stir in the shrimp and crabmeat, cook for an additional 1 minute, then remove the skillet from the heat.

• Grease 6 small ovenproof dishes with butter. Stir the cayenne pepper into the Béchamel Sauce, add the shellfish mixture and pasta, then spoon into the prepared dishes. Sprinkle with the Parmesan cheese and arrange the tomato slices on top, then brush the tomatoes with a little olive oil.

• Bake in the preheated oven for 25 minutes, or until golden brown. Serve hot with a green salad and crusty bread.

SERVES 4

1 crab, about 3 lb 5 oz/1.5 kg,
    freshly cooked
2 tbsp virgin olive oil
2 fresh red chilies, seeded
    and finely chopped
4 garlic cloves, finely chopped
1 lb 12 oz/800 g canned tomatoes
1 cup dry white wine

12 oz/350 g dried spaghetti
1 lb/450 g live mussels
2 tbsp butter
4 oz/115 g prepared raw squid, sliced
6 oz/175 g raw jumbo shrimp
3 tbsp coarsely chopped fresh
    flat-leaf parsley
1 tbsp shredded fresh basil leaves
salt and pepper

Seafood Pasta Packets

Although not a long-standing tradition, baking pockets of mixed ingredients in the oven has now become a favorite Italian cooking technique. It is especially well suited to seafood, as it seals in the moisture and keeps it tender.

• Holding the crab upright, bang it firmly on the underside of the shell with your clenched fist to loosen the body. Then, with the shell toward you and still holding it upright, force the body away from the shell by pushing with your thumbs. Twist off and discard the tail. Twist off the legs and claws. Crack them open and remove all the meat.

• Pull off and discard the gills—dead man's fingers—then split open the body down the center using a sharp knife. Remove all the meat, discarding any pieces of shell. Reserve all the shell and set the crabmeat aside. Carefully break up the larger pieces of shell with a meat mallet or the end of a rolling pin.

• Heat 1 tablespoon of the olive oil in a large pan. Add half the chilies and half the garlic, then add the pieces of crab shell. Cook over medium heat, stirring occasionally, for 2–3 minutes. Add the tomatoes with their can juices and the wine. Reduce the heat and simmer for about 1 hour. Strain the sauce, pressing down on the contents of the strainer with a wooden spoon. Season to taste with salt and pepper and reserve.

• Preheat the oven to 350°F/180°C. Bring a large pan of lightly salted water to a boil. Add the pasta, return to a boil, and cook for 8–10 minutes, until tender but still firm to the bite.

• Scrub and debeard the mussels under cold running water. Discard any damaged or broken ones and any that do not shut immediately when sharply tapped.

• Heat the remaining olive oil with the butter in a large, heavy-bottom pan. Add the remaining chili and garlic and cook over low heat, stirring occasionally, for 5 minutes, or until softened. Add the squid, shrimp, and mussels, cover, and cook over high heat for 4–5 minutes, or until the mussels have opened. Remove the pan from the heat and discard any mussels that remain closed.

• Drain the pasta and add it to the seafood with the chili and tomato sauce, parsley, and basil, tossing well to coat.

• Cut out 4 large squares of parchment paper or waxed paper. Divide the pasta and seafood among them, placing it on one half. Fold over the other half and turn in the edges securely to seal. Transfer to a large cookie sheet and bake in the preheated oven for 10 minutes, or until the pockets have puffed up. Serve immediately.

SERVES 4

olive oil, for brushing

2 eggplants, sliced

2 tbsp butter

1 garlic clove, finely chopped

4 zucchini, sliced

1 tbsp finely chopped fresh
    flat-leaf parsley

1 tbsp finely chopped fresh marjoram

8 oz/225 g mozzarella cheese, grated

2½ cups strained canned tomatoes

175 g/6 oz dried no-precook lasagna

salt and pepper

2½ cups Béchamel Sauce

½ cup freshly grated
    Parmesan cheese

Vegetarian Lasagna

Make sure that the oiled grill pan is very hot before adding the eggplant slices. Add extra oil if the eggplant is sticking to the pan.

• Preheat the oven to 400°F/200°C. Brush a large ovenproof dish with olive oil. Brush a large grill pan with olive oil and heat until smoking. Add half the eggplant slices and cook over medium heat for 8 minutes, or until golden brown all over. Remove the eggplant from the grill pan and drain on paper towels. Add the remaining eggplant slices and extra oil, if necessary, and cook for 8 minutes, or until golden brown all over.

• Melt the butter in a skillet and add the garlic, zucchini, parsley, and marjoram. Cook over medium heat, stirring frequently, for 5 minutes, or until the zucchini are golden brown all over. Remove from the skillet and let drain on paper towels.

• Layer the eggplant, zucchini, mozzarella, strained tomatoes, and lasagna in the dish, seasoning with salt and pepper as you go and finishing with a layer of lasagna. Pour over the Béchamel Sauce, making sure that all the pasta is covered. Sprinkle with the grated Parmesan cheese and bake in the preheated oven for 30–40 minutes, or until golden brown. Serve the lasagna immediately.

SERVES 4

5 oz/140 g fontina cheese,
   thinly sliced

1¼ cups hot Béchamel Sauce

6 tbsp butter, plus extra for greasing

12 oz/350 g mixed wild
   mushrooms, sliced

12 oz/350 g dried tagliatelle

2 egg yolks

4 tbsp freshly grated romano cheese

salt and pepper

mixed salad greens, to serve

Baked Pasta with Mushrooms

A bake of pasta, béchamel sauce, and a tasty filling is sometimes called a crostata.

- Preheat the oven to 400°F/200°C. Stir the fontina cheese into the Béchamel Sauce and reserve.
- Melt 2 tablespoons of the butter in a large pan. Add the mushrooms and cook over low heat, stirring occasionally, for 10 minutes.
- Meanwhile, bring a large pan of lightly salted water to a boil. Add the pasta, return to a boil, and cook for 8–10 minutes, or until tender but still firm to the bite. Drain, return to the pan, and add the remaining butter, the egg yolks, and about one-third of the sauce, then season to taste with salt and pepper. Toss well to mix, then gently stir in the mushrooms.
- Lightly grease a large, ovenproof dish with butter and spoon in the pasta mixture. Pour over the remaining sauce evenly and sprinkle with the grated romano cheese. Bake in the preheated oven for 15–20 minutes, or until golden brown. Serve immediately with mixed salad greens.

Little filled pockets of pasta, such as small or large squares or circles of ravioli, large squares of tortelloni, rings of tortellini, and crescents of agnolotti, along with stuffed tubes of cannelloni and rigatoni, are what make up filled pasta. They offer enormous possibilities for using an assortment of ingredients, such as meat, fish, vegetables, or cheese. These various filled pastas all originate in specific areas of northern and central Italy where a good supply of eggs was available to make a moist dough, suitable for stuffing. This was not the case in southern Italy, but it was from here that dried pasta originated.

You will need to make the Basic Pasta Dough recipe (see page 6) for many of the dishes in this chapter. The secret of success for making filled pasta is not to let the dough dry once it has been made, but to proceed with the recipe. Also, roll out the dough

FLAVOR FILLED

thinly, so that the shapes are not too heavy, but not so thinly that the shapes will split, and do not overfill them or they will burst when they are cooked. After making the pockets, they can be left on a clean, floured dish towel for about an hour, turning them once, so that they dry on both sides. When it comes to cooking filled pasta, try to avoid overcooking, as they may split open, which would be a pity after all your creativity!

SERVES 4

butter, for greasing

2 tbsp olive oil

2 garlic cloves, crushed

1 large onion, finely chopped

8 oz/225 g wild mushrooms, sliced

12 oz/350 g ground chicken

4 oz/115 g prosciutto, diced

2/3 cup Marsala wine

7 oz/200 g canned chopped tomatoes

1 tbsp shredded fresh basil leaves

2 tbsp tomato paste

10–12 dried cannelloni tubes

2½ cups Béchamel Sauce

¾ cup freshly grated
    Parmesan cheese

salt and pepper

Chicken and Wild Mushroom Cannelloni

You can use any combination of wild mushrooms. For extra flavor, add 1 oz/25 g dried porcini, soaked in hot water for 30 minutes.

• Preheat the oven to 375°F/190°C. Lightly grease a large ovenproof dish. Heat the olive oil in a heavy-bottom skillet. Add the garlic, onion, and mushrooms and cook over low heat, stirring frequently, for 8–10 minutes. Add the ground chicken and prosciutto and cook, stirring frequently, for 12 minutes, or until browned all over. Stir in the Marsala, tomatoes and their can juices, basil, and tomato paste and cook for 4 minutes. Season to taste with salt and pepper, then cover and simmer for 30 minutes. Uncover, stir, and simmer for 15 minutes.

• Meanwhile, bring a large, heavy-bottom pan of lightly salted water to a boil. Add the pasta, return to a boil, and cook for 8–10 minutes, or until tender but still firm to the bite. Using a slotted spoon, transfer the cannelloni tubes to a plate and pat dry with paper towels.

• Using a teaspoon, fill the cannelloni tubes with the chicken, prosciutto, and mushroom mixture. Transfer them to the ovenproof dish. Pour the Béchamel Sauce over them to cover completely and sprinkle with the grated Parmesan cheese.

• Bake the cannelloni in the preheated oven for 30 minutes, or until golden brown and bubbling. Serve immediately.

SERVES 4

4 oz/115 g skinless, boneless
   chicken breast
2 oz/55 g prosciutto
1½ oz/40 g cooked spinach,
   well drained
1 tbsp finely chopped onion

2 tbsp freshly grated
   Parmesan cheese
pinch of ground allspice
1 egg, beaten
1 lb/450 g Basic Pasta Dough
salt and pepper
2 tbsp chopped fresh flat-leaf
   parsley, to garnish

SAUCE

1¼ cups light cream
2 garlic cloves, crushed
4 oz/115 g white mushrooms,
   thinly sliced
4 tbsp freshly grated
   Parmesan cheese
salt and pepper

Chicken Tortellini

Think ahead by making double the quantity of filled tortellini. What you don't use will keep in the refrigerator for up to three days and can be used for a quick mid-week supper or snack.

• Bring a pan of lightly salted water to a boil. Add the chicken and poach for 10 minutes. Let cool slightly, then place in a food processor with the prosciutto, spinach, and onion and process until finely chopped. Stir in the Parmesan cheese, allspice, and egg and season to taste with salt and pepper.

• Thinly roll out the Pasta Dough and cut into 1½–2-inch/4–5-cm circles. Place ½ teaspoon of the chicken and ham filling in the center of each circle. Fold the pieces in half and press the edges to seal, then wrap each piece around your index finger, cross over the ends, and curl the rest of the dough backward to make a navel shape. Re-roll the trimmings and repeat until all the dough is used up.

• Bring a pan of salted water to a boil. Add the tortellini, in batches, return to a boil, and cook for 5 minutes. Drain the tortellini well and transfer to a serving dish.

• To make the sauce, bring the cream and garlic to a boil in a small pan, then simmer for 3 minutes. Add the mushrooms and half the cheese, season to taste with salt and pepper, and simmer for 2–3 minutes. Pour the sauce over the tortellini. Sprinkle over the remaining Parmesan cheese, garnish with the parsley, and serve.

SERVES 4

2 tbsp olive oil

2 onions, chopped

2 garlic cloves, finely chopped

1 tbsp shredded fresh basil

1 lb 12 oz/800 g chopped tomatoes

1 tbsp tomato paste

12 oz/350 g dried cannelloni tubes

butter, for greasing

1 cup ricotta cheese

4 oz/115 g cooked ham, diced

1 egg

½ cup freshly grated romano cheese

salt and pepper

Cannelloni with Ham and Ricotta

Make sure that the cooked cannelloni tubes are dry before filling, as they may go soggy during cooking. Pat dry thoroughly with paper towels before filling with the ham and ricotta mixture.

• Preheat the oven to 350°F/180°C. Heat the olive oil in a large, heavy-bottom skillet. Add the onions and garlic and cook over low heat, stirring occasionally, for 5 minutes, or until the onion is softened. Add the basil, chopped tomatoes and their can juices, and tomato paste and season to taste with salt and pepper. Reduce the heat and let simmer for 30 minutes, or until thickened.

• Meanwhile, bring a large, heavy-bottom pan of lightly salted water to a boil. Add the dried cannelloni tubes, return to a boil, and cook for 8–10 minutes, or until tender but still firm to the bite. Using a slotted spoon, transfer the cannelloni tubes to a large plate and pat dry with paper towels.

• Grease a large, shallow ovenproof dish with butter. Mix the ricotta, ham, and egg together in a bowl and season to taste with salt and pepper. Using a teaspoon, fill the cannelloni tubes with the ricotta, ham, and egg mixture and place in a single layer in the dish. Pour the tomato sauce over the cannelloni and sprinkle with the grated romano cheese. Bake in the preheated oven for 30 minutes, or until golden brown. Serve immediately.

SERVES 4

4 oz/115 g cooked skinless, boneless
   chicken breast, coarsely chopped
2 oz/55 g cooked spinach
2 oz/55 g prosciutto,
   coarsely chopped
1 shallot, coarsely chopped

6 tbsp freshly grated romano cheese
pinch of freshly grated nutmeg
2 eggs, lightly beaten
1 quantity Basic Pasta Dough
all-purpose flour, for dusting
1¼ cups heavy cream
   or panna da cucina

2 garlic cloves, finely chopped
4 oz/115 g cremini mushrooms,
   thinly sliced
2 tbsp shredded fresh basil
salt and pepper
fresh basil sprigs, to garnish

Creamy Chicken Ravioli

To cook the chicken breast, place it in a pan with 1 tablespoon lemon juice and just enough water to cover. Season to taste with salt and pepper and poach gently for 10 minutes, or until cooked.

• Place the chicken, spinach, prosciutto, and shallot in a food processor and process until chopped and blended. Transfer to a bowl, stir in 2 tablespoons of the romano cheese, the nutmeg, and half the egg. Season to taste with salt and pepper.

• Halve the Pasta Dough. Wrap one piece in plastic wrap and thinly roll out the other on a lightly floured counter. Cover with a dish towel and roll out the second piece of dough. Place small mounds of the filling in rows 1½ inches/ 4 cm apart on one sheet of dough and brush the spaces in between with beaten egg. Lift the second piece of dough to fit on top. Press down firmly between the mounds of filling, pushing out any air. Cut into squares and place on a floured dish towel. Let the ravioli rest for 1 hour.

• Bring a large pan of lightly salted water to a boil. Add the ravioli, in batches, return to a boil, and cook for 5 minutes. Remove with a slotted spoon and drain on paper towels, then transfer to a warmed dish.

• Meanwhile, to make the sauce, pour the cream into a skillet, add the garlic, and bring to a boil. Simmer for 1 minute, then add the mushrooms and 2 tablespoons of the remaining cheese. Season to taste and simmer for 3 minutes. Stir in the basil, then pour the sauce over the ravioli. Sprinkle with the remaining cheese, garnish with basil sprigs, and serve.

SERVES 4

butter, for greasing

1 lb/450 g dried rigatoni

4 oz/115 g sun-dried tomatoes
   in oil, drained and sliced

FILLING

7 oz/200 g canned flaked tuna,
   drained

1 cup ricotta cheese

SAUCE

½ cup heavy cream

2 cups freshly grated
   Parmesan cheese

salt and pepper

Baked Tuna and Ricotta Rigatoni

For a vegetarian alternative, simply substitute a mixture of pitted and chopped black olives and chopped walnuts for the tuna. Follow exactly the same cooking method.

• Preheat the oven to 400°F/200°C. Lightly grease a large ovenproof dish with butter. Bring a large, heavy-bottom pan of lightly salted water to a boil. Add the rigatoni, return to a boil, and cook for 8–10 minutes, or until just tender but still firm to the bite. Drain the pasta and let stand until cool enough to handle.

• Meanwhile, mix the tuna and ricotta cheese together in a bowl to form a soft paste. Spoon the mixture into a pastry bag and use to fill the rigatoni. Arrange the filled pasta tubes side by side in the prepared dish.

• To make the sauce, mix the cream and Parmesan cheese together in a bowl and season to taste with salt and pepper. Spoon the sauce over the rigatoni and top with the sun-dried tomatoes, arranged in a criss-cross pattern. Bake in the preheated oven for 20 minutes. Serve hot straight from the dish.

SERVES 4
12 dried cannelloni tubes,
   3 inches/7.5 cm long
butter, for greasing

FILLING
5 oz/140 g cooked lean ham, chopped
5 oz/140 g frozen spinach, thawed
   and drained
½ cup ricotta cheese
1 egg
3 tbsp freshly grated romano cheese
pinch of freshly grated nutmeg
salt and pepper

CHEESE SAUCE
2½ cups milk
2 tbsp unsalted butter
2 tbsp all-purpose flour
¾ cup freshly grated Gruyère cheese
salt and pepper

Cannelloni with Spinach and Ricotta

Cannelloni started life as sheets of rectangular pasta (lasagna), which were rolled around a filling, but now large tubes of pasta, ready for stuffing with your favorite filling, are available.

• Preheat the oven to 350°F/180°C. Bring a large pan of lightly salted water to a boil. Add the cannelloni tubes, return to a boil, and cook for 6–7 minutes, or until nearly tender. Drain and rinse under cold water. Spread out the tubes on a clean dish towel.

• Place the ham, spinach, and ricotta in a food processor and process for a few seconds until combined. Add the egg and romano cheese and process again to a smooth paste. Transfer to a bowl and season with nutmeg, salt, and pepper.

• Grease an ovenproof dish with butter. Spoon the filling into a pastry bag fitted with a ½-inch/1-cm tip. Carefully open one cannelloni tube, stand it upright, and pipe in the filling. Place the filled tube in the dish and continue to fill the remaining cannelloni.

• To make the Cheese Sauce, heat the milk to just below boiling point. Meanwhile, melt the butter in a separate pan. Add the flour to the butter and cook over low heat, stirring constantly, for 1 minute. Remove the pan from the heat and gradually stir in the hot milk. Return the pan to the heat and bring to a boil, stirring constantly. Simmer over the lowest possible heat, stirring frequently, for 10 minutes until thickened and smooth. Remove the pan from the heat, stir in the Gruyère cheese, and season to taste with salt and pepper.

• Spoon the Cheese Sauce over the filled cannelloni. Cover the dish with foil and bake in the preheated oven for 20–25 minutes. Serve immediately.

SERVES 4

6 scallions

12 oz/350 g cooked crabmeat

2 tsp finely chopped fresh gingerroot

⅛–¼ tsp chili or Tabasco sauce

1 lb 9 oz/700 g tomatoes, peeled,
seeded, and coarsely chopped

1 garlic clove, finely chopped

1 tbsp white wine vinegar

1 quantity Basic Pasta Dough

all-purpose flour, for dusting

1 egg, lightly beaten

2 tbsp heavy cream or
panna da cucina

salt

shredded scallion, to garnish

Crab Ravioli

For a change, use
tomato-, beet-, or
spinach-flavored
pasta instead of
the plain variety.

• Thinly slice the scallions, keeping the white and green parts separate. Mix the green scallions, crabmeat, ginger, and chili sauce to taste together in a bowl. Cover with plastic wrap and chill.

• Place the tomatoes in a food processor and process to a purée. Place the garlic, white scallions, and vinegar in a pan and add the puréed tomatoes. Bring to a boil, stirring frequently, then reduce the heat and simmer gently for 10 minutes. Remove from the heat.

• Halve the Pasta Dough. Wrap one piece in plastic wrap and thinly roll out the other on a lightly floured work surface. Cover with a tea towel and roll out the second piece of dough. Place small mounds of the crabmeat mixture in rows 1½ inches/4 cm apart on one sheet of dough and brush the spaces in between with beaten egg. Lift the second piece of dough to fit on top. Press down firmly between the mounds of filling, pushing out any air. Cut into squares, place on a dish towel and let rest for 1 hour.

• Bring a large, heavy-bottom pan of lightly salted water to a boil. Add the ravioli, in batches, return to a boil, and cook for 5 minutes. Remove with a slotted spoon and drain on paper towels. Meanwhile, gently heat the tomato sauce and whisk in the cream. Place the ravioli in serving dishes, pour over the sauce, garnish with shredded scallion, and serve.

SERVES 4

butter, for greasing

1 quantity Basic Pasta Dough

all-purpose flour, for dusting

¾ cup freshly grated
    Parmesan cheese

mixed salad greens, to serve

FILLING

½ cup olive oil

1 red onion, chopped

3 garlic cloves, chopped

2 large eggplants, cut into chunks

3 large zucchini, cut into chunks

6 beefsteak tomatoes, peeled,
    seeded, and coarsely chopped

1 large green bell pepper,
    seeded and diced

1 large red bell pepper,
    seeded and diced

1 tbsp sun-dried tomato paste

1 tbsp shredded fresh basil

salt and pepper

Mixed Vegetable Agnolotti

If the filling seems too sloppy after cooking, boil uncovered for 1–2 minutes to reduce slightly. Make sure that any unused dough is covered with a dish towel to prevent it drying out.

• Preheat the oven to 400°F/200°C. To make the filling, heat the olive oil in a large, heavy-bottom pan. Add the onion and garlic and cook over low heat, stirring occasionally, for 5 minutes, or until softened. Add the eggplant, zucchini, tomatoes, green and red bell peppers, sun-dried tomato paste, and basil. Season to taste with salt and pepper, cover, and let simmer gently, stirring occasionally, for 20 minutes.

• Lightly grease an ovenproof dish with butter. Roll out the Pasta Dough on a lightly floured counter and stamp out 3-inch/7.5-cm circles with a plain cutter. Place a spoonful of the vegetable filling on one side of each circle. Dampen the edges slightly and fold the pasta circles over, pressing together to seal.

• Bring a large pan of lightly salted water to a boil. Add the agnolotti, in batches if necessary, return to a boil, and cook for 3–4 minutes. Remove with a slotted spoon, drain, and transfer to the dish. Sprinkle with the Parmesan cheese and bake in the preheated oven for 20 minutes. Serve with salad greens.

SERVES 4

12 dried cannelloni tubes

4 tbsp olive oil, plus extra
for brushing

2 tbsp butter

1 lb/450 g mixed wild mushrooms,
finely chopped

1 garlic clove, finely chopped

1½ cups fresh bread crumbs

⅔ cup milk

1 cup ricotta cheese

6 tbsp freshly grated
Parmesan cheese

2 tbsp pine nuts

2 tbsp slivered almonds

salt and pepper

TOMATO SAUCE

2 tbsp olive oil

1 onion, finely chopped

1 garlic clove, finely chopped

1 lb 12 oz/800 g canned
chopped tomatoes

1 tbsp tomato paste

8 black olives, pitted and chopped

salt and pepper

Mushroom Cannelloni

Use either a teaspoon or a pastry bag fitted with a large plain tip to fill the cannelloni tubes. Do not overfill them.

• Preheat the oven to 375°F/190°C. Bring a large pan of lightly salted water to a boil. Add the cannelloni tubes, return to a boil, and cook for 8–10 minutes, or until tender but still firm to the bite. With a slotted spoon, transfer the cannelloni tubes to a plate and pat dry. Brush a large ovenproof dish with olive oil.

• Meanwhile, make the Tomato Sauce. Heat the olive oil in a skillet. Add the onion and garlic and cook over low heat for 5 minutes, or until softened. Add the tomatoes and their can juices, tomato paste, and olives and season to taste with salt and pepper. Bring to a boil and cook for 3–4 minutes. Pour the sauce into the ovenproof dish.

• To make the filling, melt the butter in a heavy-bottom skillet. Add the mushrooms and garlic and cook over medium heat, stirring frequently, for 3–5 minutes, or until tender. Remove the skillet from the heat. Mix the bread crumbs, milk, and olive oil together in a large bowl, then stir in the ricotta, mushroom mixture, and 4 tablespoons of the Parmesan cheese. Season to taste with salt and pepper.

• Fill the cannelloni tubes with the mushroom mixture and place them in the dish. Brush with olive oil and sprinkle with the remaining Parmesan cheese, pine nuts, and almonds. Bake in the oven for 25 minutes, or until golden.

SERVES 4

12 oz/350 g spinach leaves,
coarse stalks removed

1 cup ricotta cheese

½ cup freshly grated
Parmesan cheese

2 eggs, lightly beaten

pinch of freshly grated nutmeg

1 quantity Spinach Pasta Dough

all-purpose flour, for dusting

pepper

TO SERVE

freshly grated Parmesan
cheese (optional)

Cheese Sauce or Tomato Sauce
(optional)

Spinach and Ricotta Ravioli

When cutting the ravioli into squares, use a special pasta cutter available from specialty kitchenware stores. Alternatively, you can use a sharp knife.

• Cook the spinach, with just the water clinging to the leaves after washing, over low heat for 5 minutes until wilted. Drain and squeeze out as much moisture as possible. Cool, then chop finely. Beat the ricotta cheese until smooth, then stir in the spinach, Parmesan, and half the egg and season to taste with nutmeg and pepper.

• Halve the Pasta Dough. Cover one piece and thinly roll out the other on a floured counter. Cover and roll out the second piece. Put small mounds of filling in rows 1½ inches/4 cm apart on one sheet of dough and brush the spaces in between with the remaining beaten egg. Lift the second piece of dough to fit on top. Press down between the mounds, pushing out any air. Cut into squares and rest on a dish towel for 1 hour.

• Bring a large pan of salted water to a boil, add the ravioli, in batches, return to a boil, and cook for 5 minutes. Remove with a slotted spoon and drain on paper towels. Serve with grated Parmesan cheese and/or a sauce.

Index